Ants

Contents

Is it a monster?	2
Fantastic nests	4
Meet the queen	6
Ants kill	8
Smart ants	10
Fantastic ants	12
Ant antics!	22

Written by Danny Pearson

Collins

Is it a monster?

You might think ants are little and **harmless**.

But ants are strong and smart.

Fantastic nests

Lots of ants have nests in the soil.

This ant constructs a nest in the treetops with silk.

Wood ants construct **vents** in the nest to let out hot air!

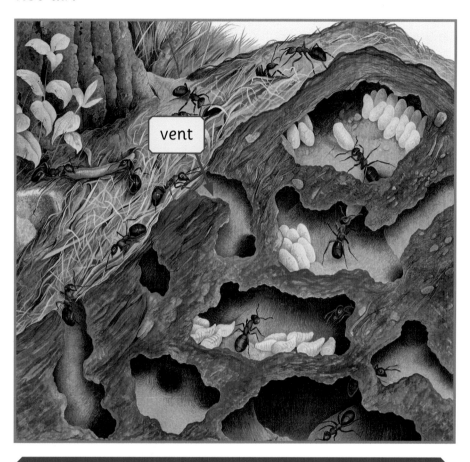

vent

Fact!
This silver ant nests in the sand.

Meet the queen

In this crowded ants' nest, there is one queen.
All the eggs come from her.

6

The rest of the ants bring her food, such as sweet **sap** and grains.

Ants kill

Ants can attack bigger insects for food.

Some ants can kill snails, frogs and toads.

A trail of ants marches up a tree looking for food in the treetop.

This ant is little, but has big nippers.

Fact!
A wood ant defends itself with stinging liquid.

Smart ants

Ants can cling together to form a sort of boat that floats so they do not drown.

Look at this ant's foot. The hairs grab onto bark to help them cling on.

Fantastic ants

Ants are strong. They can **hoist** things up that are much bigger than them.

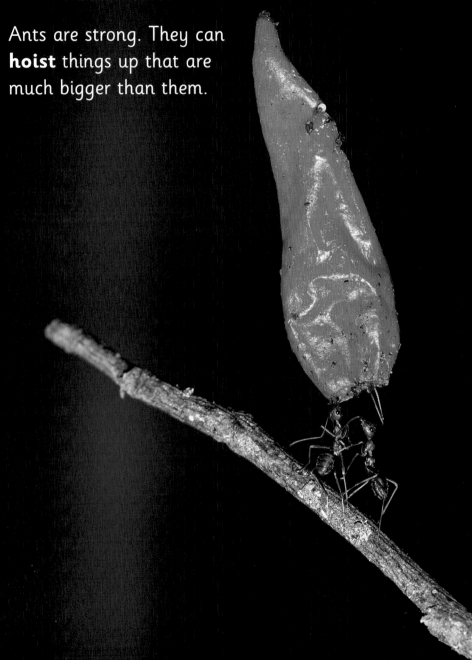

Some ants can swoop at speed too!

harmless not going to hurt you

hoist lift up

sap sweet liquid from trees

vents gaps that let air in and out

Index

eggs 6, 16
queen 6, 16
silk 4
silver ant 5, 19
vents 5
wood ant 5, 9, 18

Ant nest

ant eggs

queen

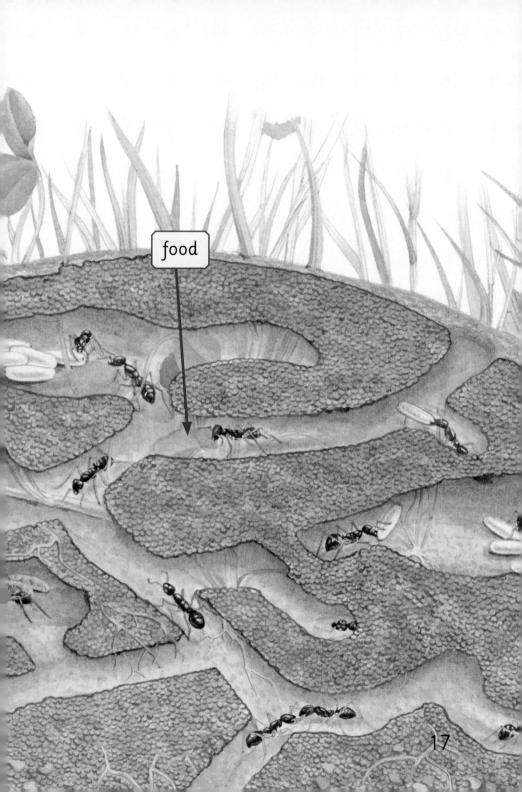

food

Ant breeds

red wood ant

green ant

brown ant

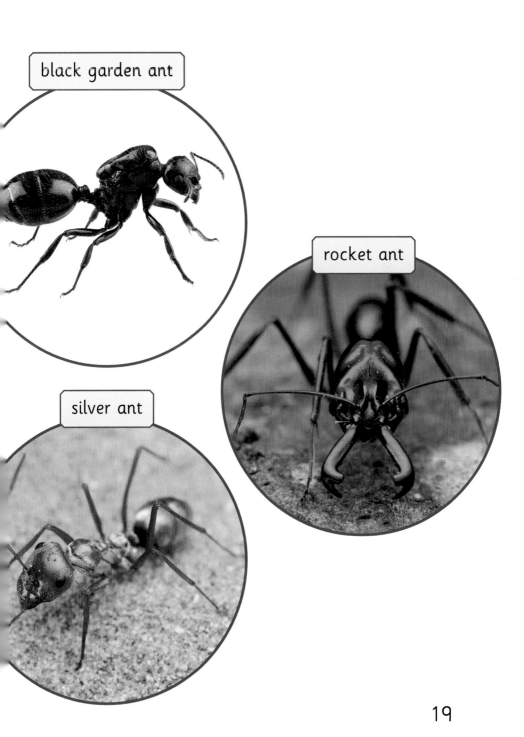

black garden ant

rocket ant

silver ant

19

Biggest ant

Littlest ant

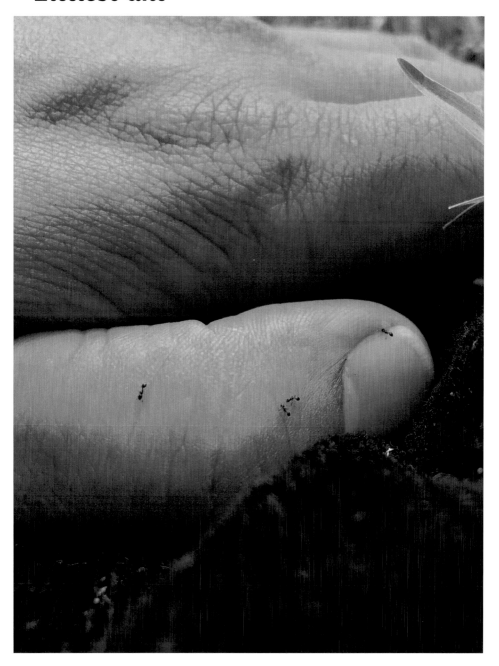

Ant antics!

Review: After reading

Use your assessment from hearing the children read to choose any GPCs, words or tricky words that need additional practice.

Read 1: Decoding

- Turn to page 11 and point to the word **bark**. Say: **bark** can be the noise a dog makes. How do we know a dog bark isn't meant here? If necessary, explain that **bark** can also mean the outer layer of a tree.

- Encourage the children to practise sounding out longer words and to look out for long vowel sounds, too. Say: Sound out these words – they all have one long vowel sound in them.

  h/ar/m/less   s/m/ar/t   t/r/ee/t/o/p/s   s/i/l/v/er   t/r/ai/l   f/l/oa/t/s

- Challenge the children to read the contents list fluently. Say: Can you blend in your head when you read these words?

Read 2: Prosody

- Model reading page 8 as if you are presenting a nature documentary.

- Ask the children to take over, reading page 9 with the same enthusiasm and expression. Suggest they introduce the "Fact" in their own words.

Read 3: Comprehension

- Ask the children to describe any ants they have seen in real life or on television. Ask: Were they like any of the ants in the book? How?

- Ask the children how they think the author feels about ants. Encourage them to point to evidence in the text such as the repetition of **Fantastic** in the contents list.

- Discuss how you can find information quickly. For example:

  o On page 5, ask: How do I find out what **vents** means? (*turn to the glossary on page 14*)

  o Ask: How do I find the pages that cover ants nests? (*turn to the Contents*)

  o Ask: If I want to find the page that talks about a specific ant – like the silver ant – where should I look? (*the Index*)

- Look together at pages 22 and 23. Talk about what the ants are doing in each picture. Check that the children understand what "antics" means (e.g. *things the ants get up to*).

- Bonus content: Ask the children to prepare a few things to say about pages 16 and 17. Can they identify things in the illustration?